WINSTON CHURCHILL

THE HISTORY HOUR

CONTENTS

PART I
Introduction — 1

PART II
THE BEGINNING: A LOOK AT WINSTON CHURCHILL'S CHILDHOOD, MILITARY CAREER, AND AS AN AUTHOR

The Beginning Steps to Greatness: The Earliest Years — 5

Churchill's Great Escape — 11

Churchill's Hat of Authorship — 14

PART III
WINSTON CHURCHILL, FAMILY MAN, AND POLITICS

The Great and Not So Great Friendships — 21

The Political Beginnings of a Political Star — 25

A Political Family Man — 28

Women's Rights and other Social Causes — 32

PART IV
THE LATER YEARS OF SIR WINSTON CHURCHILL

The Start of the Second World War — 41

Churchill and the 1940s — 47

The Retirement Years of Churchill — 56

PART V
Conclusion — 59

PART VI
For Further Reading... — 63

PART VII
Bibliography — 65

Your Free eBook! — 67

Copyright © 2018 by Kolme Korkeudet Oy

All rights reserved.

No part of this book may be reproduced in any form or by any electronic or mechanical means, including information storage and retrieval systems, without written permission from the author, except for the use of brief quotations in a book review.

I
INTRODUCTION

❧

Success is not final, failure is not fatal: it is the courage to continue that counts.
Winston Churchill

❧

Sir Winston Churchill's funeral was known to be one of the grandest funerals which Great Britain could give him. It has been fifty years since his passing, and he is still one of the most discussed historical figures in many areas of the world, including England and the United States. During his life, Winston had obtained honor in several areas as he was a historian, politician, statesman, parliamentarian, journalist, soldier, and painter. Even with all of his accomplishments, he still is a man who does not often receive the credit he deserves. Part of the reason for this is because it is so hard to grasp the many areas of Churchill's life, especially when looking at the length and accomplishments of his political career. Many people call Churchill one of the last great historians while others discuss his political career, which is the area of his life he is most known for. His political career spanned from about 1900 and well into the 1940s, which saw him face two wars and varying social changes. In his early years, Winston Churchill wanted to prove he was more than just a son of aristocratic parents.

II

THE BEGINNING: A LOOK AT WINSTON CHURCHILL'S CHILDHOOD, MILITARY CAREER, AND AS AN AUTHOR

❦

Success is not final, failure is not fatal: it is the courage to continue that counts.
Winston Churchill

THE BEGINNING STEPS TO GREATNESS: THE EARLIEST YEARS

❦

Winston Churchill did not speak of his childhood much but did lead to the fact that it was lonely and miserable. Winston Leonard Spencer Churchill was born in Blenheim Palace, Oxfordshire, England on November 30, 1874. His father was Lord Randolph Churchill, who was a British statesman. Winston's mother, Jeanette "Jennie" Jerome, was originally a New York City Socialite. From the beginning, Churchill's life showed promise as he lived a life of privilege, being born into an established English family, a family of aristocracy. Churchill's grandfather was the seventh Duke of Marlborough. From the outside, it seemed that Winston Churchill lived the perfect aristocratic life. However, while his parents were socially well-established, they were generally distant and did not have a lot of financial security. Both sets of Winston's grandparents would support his parents throughout his life as they often found themselves in debt. Furthermore, Winston Churchill's parents were distant from their children. Because of this,

Churchill childhood was known to be unhappy and neglected, except for the care of nurture of his nanny, Mrs. Everest. Winston, and his younger brother, Jack, would often travel with Mrs. Everest (who was not married but given the honorary title as 'Mrs.') between the homes of their parents and grandparents. In his later years, Churchill would reflect on the loneliness of his childhood by stating that he would find joy internally and often turned to reading, which helped in filling up the void of loneliness.

※

While living in Dublin, Ireland, Churchill became a somewhat rebellious and independent individual. As was customary for his lifestyle, Winston was sent to boarding schools. In his first two schools, Churchill did not do well, even though he often wrote to his parents discussing how much he enjoyed school. Winston Churchill would admit in his later life that he, in fact, hated school and did not enjoy going to his earlier schools, with one being St. George's School.

※

Winston was in early elementary school when he attended St. George's School, which was a horrifying experience for the boy from day one. After the first session was over, Winston's parents would learn the truth about their son's educational matters as St. George's school, when they received a letter with the remarks that Winston needed to take his education more seriously. The poor experience Winston felt at St. George's School only grew through the poor treatment he received, being cited as one of the naughtiest boys in the school and often receiving beatings. Even for the age in which

Churchill lived, St. George's School was known to be extremely harsh in their discipline and handle of the student body. The mix of cruel treatment and lack of interest in several subjects of study creating a crushing beginning for Winston at St. George's school. However, within a year of attending the school, the Head Master did begin to see a bit of improvement in Winston, claiming that while he was still one of the most rebellious kids in the school, he seemed to be improving, but there was still much improvement needing to be done.

❧

Another boarding school, which Churchill began attending in the late 1880s called Harrow School, would become one of the first steps he took towards his life military and political life as Sir Winston Churchill. Within the first year of life at Harrow School, Churchill decided to join the Harrow Rifle Corps, which opened the door to his military career. However, the profession did not take off without first having the struggle of getting it started.

❧

It is believed that one reason Winston chose the military over more suitable roles for his social status was due to his poor performance in school. Whatever the case might be, the road that Winston chose in attending the Royal Military College become the correct road for his path. Unfortunately, the road started off rocky as it took three times for Winston to pass the entrance exam. And once he did pass, he only passed enough to be able to enter under the Calvary division and not the Infantry division. For Winston, he was pleased with his role in the Calvary and hoped that this would be something which would make his father proud of him. However, Winston would later find out that Lord Randolph was disappointed that his son did not make the Infantry division.

❧

It was also at the Royal Military College where Winston finally saw the grades that his parents had hoped for while he was a child. During his time at the university, Winston was able to take courses which interested him, and he found his subjects exciting. Before, he felt handicapped by the foreign languages, especially Latin as he never saw the point of studying a language he would never use. At the university, he was no longer handicapped by Latin, French, and mathematics. Instead, he could focus more on history, mapmaking, military law, drill, and riding. If Winston did not prove he was not only intelligent and hardworking during his courses at the Royal Military College, he definitely showed it at the graduation. Instead of being one of the lowest students in his class, which was the case in his childhood, he graduated from the university 20th out of 130 students.

❧

From joining the military to becoming one of the most exceptional speakers of all time, Winston Churchill held many roles during his lifetime. One reason he held so many positions from author to Prime Minister during a time of war was because he was a man of great strength. He was confident and stubborn in his values and believed things should be a certain way, but this never stopped him from listening to the other side of the discussion and trying to understand people at their beliefs and levels. Even if his father could not fully see it during his lifetime, Winston Churchill was a great man with high intelligence for politics and profound observation, which would help him throughout his career

❦

Unfortunately, by the time Churchill was to put on a uniform in a way that was sure to make his father proud, Lord Randolph passed away on January 24, 1895. Within a few months after this event, Winston saw himself in the 4th Queen's Own Hussars as a Calvary officer. But Winston Churchill did not see the success of a war hero until about four years later when he returned home after escaping the Boer POW camp. It was then that Winston's military career took off in the path that not only made Winston proud but would have made his father proud as well.

Winston Churchill made his first political speech in the summer of 1897. While it did not make him a political star, this would come much later in his career, he was pleased with the journalist's report on his speech. However, during that same summer, Churchill and his friend, Sir Bindon Blood, went off to India for the war which had broken out. While being there, waiting to hear from Blood, Winston wrote to his mother that the temperature was well over 100 degrees. When word did come from Blood, Winston was disappointed because Blood informed him that he could not appoint Winston as his staff because they were friends. Therefore, Winston went to where Blood was stationed as a war correspondent with the hope that he would one day be appointed as one of Blood's men.

❦

Winston went on to meet Blood at Camp Malakand, where he began writing about his time stationed there to the Daily Telegraph. He also wrote letters, which were unsigned, to the Pioneer Mail. He also continued writing to his brother and mother, mentioning that his time in the military would surely give him a foot in the door politically. He further wrote to his mother that he had to act in certain ways, such as take risks he usually would not, to be noted by Blood's superiors and staff.

CHURCHILL'S GREAT ESCAPE

※

During the late 1890s, Churchill spent his time between England and India, focusing on writing, his political career, and his military roles. However, it was not until the fall of 1899 when Churchill would become the individual he often desired to be. During the Anglo-Boer War, Churchill was a correspondent, who wrote articles for The Morning Post, only a couple days after the war started. Within two weeks, Churchill was captured and held as a Boer war prisoner. While Churchill was not technically ready for combat during the attack on the train, he offered up to help the conductor and ran around trying to find and help load the wounded onto a train so they could get to a safe destination and be taken care of. It was during this time that the wounded began to see Churchill as a hero. However, he also made a mistake by leaving his gun on the seat of the railroad car, so when the Boer attacked Churchill, he was unarmed. In his novel, My Early Life, Churchill described his attack by writing,

> *"I thought there was absolutely no chance of an escape; if he fired, he would surely hit me, so I held up my hands and surrendered myself a prisoner of war. 'When one is alone and unarmed,' said the great Napoleon, in words which flowed into my mind in the poignant minutes that followed, 'a surrender may be pardoned.'"*

❧

At first, Churchill tried to be released as a prisoner by telling the Boers he was not in combat. However, the Boers did not believe Churchill because they had read his heroin reports about him during the attack on the train. Unable to be freed voluntarily, Churchill began his plan of escape. Joining in a plan of actions where others would try to escape as well, Churchill was the first prisoner out the window and over the fence. He was also the only prisoner to be able to escape successfully. People quickly learned about Churchill's escape as the Boers stated they were offering a £25 reward for him "dead or alive."

❧

Of course, the story about his escape and the reward only made the rest of Churchill's escape a more significant challenge as while he safely made it over 70 miles from the prison, he was still around 200 miles away from the Indian frontier. Fortunately, for Churchill, he was able to befriend a British coal miner by the name of John Howard, who hid him within the coal mines until one of Howard's friends, a shopkeeper by the name of Charles Burnham was able to sneak him onto a train and get Churchill to safety. It was once Churchill landed to safety that he learned he had become a celebrity through his heroic efforts on the train and his escape from the Boer prison camp. When Churchill finally arrived home on the streets of England the summer of 1900, he was greeted as a hero. As he had written to his family before, he had hoped that his time in the military would bring him enough social notice to be able to achieve a political career fully. However, it was not just his military career that gave him notice but also the writing and publishing he did while he was working in the military. While wearing his hat as an army correspondent, Churchill also worked on his career as an author.

CHURCHILL'S HAT OF AUTHORSHIP

❦

Winston Churchill first became a published author in 1898 with his book The Story of the Malakand Field Force. While working under Sir Bindon Blood on the Indian Frontier as a correspondent, Churchill wrote about his story and life in this setting. Slowly, the book began to make waves in society. It was not long after the publishing of this book that Churchill furthered his writing career by publishing his second book, The River War, a year later. This book was similar to the first one as it told about his time as a war correspondent. In 1900, Churchill wrote a novel titled, Savrola, which is Churchill's political philosophy written in as a fictional adventure. Different from his first two books, which were basically memoirs, this was Churchill's first and what would be his only novel in his long lists of published books.

❦

Winston Churchill remained a busy author in 1900 as Savrola was not his only published work. He also published two more books, first of which was London to Lady Smith and then he published Ian Hamilton's March. After 1900, Churchill took a three-year break in publishing, not coming out with his next book until 1903, with Mr. Brodrick's Army. In 1906, Churchill paid tribute to his father by writing the two-volume book Lord Randolph Churchill, which basically defended his father's reputation. In many ways, writing a book in defense of his father was a big step in closing any unresolved issues Churchill had with his father. In his earlier life, Churchill felt he knew his father more through his reputation than actually being able to personally get to know him because the two were so distant. On top of the book about his father, Churchill also published a 136-page book consisting of nine speeches titled For Free Trade. It would be another two years before Winston Churchill would continue making waves in the world of being an author.

From 1908 until 1910, Winston Churchill published a book every year starting with My African Journey and the following year with Liberalism and the Social Problem. Published in 1909, this book became Winston Churchill's first hard covered book. Winston Churchill then went on to publish a book, containing six speeches from the General Election reprimanding the Tories for their refusal of The People's Budget, simply and appropriately titled, The People's Right. Today, this book is known to be one of the rarest books of Winston Churchill's collection to find.

Winston Churchill took over a decade before returning to the publisher after The People's Choice. It was not until 1923 when Churchill began publishing his five-volume set titled The World Crisis. He never finished publishing this set until 1931. The books discuss the history of World War One. While he worked on the series for about eight years, during this time Winston also published two other books with one being a biography about himself simply titled, My Early Years, which was published in 1930. This book is the best way to learn about Churchill's early life, especially his childhood. Furthermore, it is the only book in which Churchill wrote detailing his personal memoirs. Churchill also published his book India in 1931 which is a series of speeches about the duty in India and Gandhi. In 1932, Churchill went back in time, which he often did as a historian, and published a book titled Thoughts and Adventures which is a collection of his 1920s and 1930s magazine articles and essays.

Winston Churchill continued his writing as a biographer from 1933 until 1938 with his initial four-volume set of books about his grandfather, John Churchill, called Malborough: His Life and Times. During these years, he also published the Great Contemporaries in 1937 and Arms and the Covenant in 1938. He then finished the 1930s with his publication of Step by Step in 1939. This book was one of Churchill's first steps in trying to fight the Nazi uprising and Hitler, which would also become a big focus during his political career.

During the 1940s, Winston Churchill further grew his writing and publishing career, starting with the seven-volume set of speeches called The War Speeches. Churchill began publishing this set in 1941 and finished in 1946. 1948 became a big year for Churchill's writing career as he not only started publishing The Second World War six-volume series, which ended in 1953, but he also began publishing The Post War Speeches. This series is a five-volume set, which was published until 1961. On top of starting off these two series of books, Winston Churchill also published a book called Painting as a Pastime. This was actually an essay discussing Winston Churchill's first hobby and was first published in two parts in a magazine called Strand in the early 1920s and then as part of his book, Thoughts and Adventures, before officially becoming published as its own book in 1948.

※

During Winston Churchill's later years, he published a bit less than he had before. In 1956, he turned back to his historian roots and began publishing A History of the English Speaking Peoples, which was a four-volume history on England. It detailed several areas of England's history, such as the colonies and the English language. The series was completed two years later, with the last one published in 1958. The only book Winston Churchill would publish in the 1960s was in 1962 and called Frontiers and Wars. This would be the last book published in Churchill's lifetime. However, this does not mean that more books were not published later. Along with the help of editors, Churchill's Young Winston's Wars, which is about the colonial wars in India was published in 1972 and then If I Lived My Life Again in 1974. Furthermore, Churchill has a posthumous series written by him called Post-humous Collected Editions, which were published between

1974 and 2003. These works are six of Winston Churchill's speeches and writings which have been reprinted.

※

With such a long and varied writing and publishing career, Churchill led that role well throughout his life. However, one of the most prominent roles during Winston Churchill's career was his career as a politician.

❧ III ☙
WINSTON CHURCHILL, FAMILY MAN, AND POLITICS

☙☙

Attitude is a little thing that makes a big difference.
Winston Churchill

☙☙

The active political career of Winston Churchill began in 1900 when he was elected to the House of Commons, winning an Oldham seat. It was also around this time when Churchill started changing his political views, mostly because of his time in the military. Before this time, Churchill mainly followed the views of conservatives, however, due to the issue he had seen while in the military and war, he began to change his views to better issues within the military area. This meant that Winston Churchill was still conservative, but he also tended to include some liberal sympathies in his political views. And this would not be the last time that Winston Churchill would change his political views or even parties.

※

Through his political career, Churchill did many things such as public speaking. Churchill was a grand speaker, and not only he knew it, but those around him, those who went to hear him, and many who heard of him also knew it. Throughout his career, he gave dozens of speeches, many of which would eventually make it to be published in a few of his books. And Churchill wasted no time in beginning his public speaking career as once he was elected into Oldham, he started touring as a public speaker. During this time, he would travel throughout Great Britain and the United States of America, earning himself about £10,000. But while Winston Churchill would spend much of his political life speaking, his most famous speeches were all actually done within a few months of each other. These speeches were also closer to the middle to end of Winston Churchill's political career, around the time of the Second World War, which we will discuss later in this chapter.

THE GREAT AND NOT SO GREAT FRIENDSHIPS

❧

Not only did Winston Churchill build up his career as a public speaker immediately after being elected, but he also began to form some really good friendships with others in the public office. However, he also started to make enemies. Churchill was very passionate about his views and something this passion would take over, and it would not agree with other political views of other politicians. Winston Churchill was a man who knew what he believed. He was a man who knew when he was right about an opinion, he was right, and he was not afraid to state so. For many, this could often come off and a bit of crude behavior. One such example of this would be Winston Churchill's complicated relationship with Gandhi.

❧

While part of Churchill's complicated relationship with Gandhi had to do with Gandhi's belief against British rule, the relationship ran a bit deeper than that. In fact, this relationship between the two was so strong that it ended up changing the path of the countries, and in a sense, ended up changing history. But their relationship also has a personal twist due to the fact they were different and yet their careers were similar. Churchill, as I have written about previously, was born into an aristocratic family, even though he lived poorly and did not inherit any wealth from his parents. Mohandas Gandhi, on the other hand, grew up in an Indian middle-class household. However, both men would guide their nations through some tough times of the twentieth century, which would include two wars for both of them. Furthermore, they would both become highly important figures in not only the history of their nations but also world history. One of the best ways to learn the details of their very complicated relationship is to read Arthur Herman's book, *Gandhi & Churchill: The Epic Rivalry that Destroyed an Empire and Forged Our Age*, which was published in 2009. The really lovely treat about Arthur Herman's book is it is not a comparable side by side biography of Churchill and Gandhi. Instead, the book includes several short facts about the two men and then digs deeper into their views, the accomplishments they made, and then looks at what and why the views of the men creating such a historical relationship. For instance, the book describes that Churchill did not support Gandhi's beliefs of having Indian independence because, as Churchill believed, this would have a lot of negative consequences and, of course, bloodshed. While the book does lead to looking into more of how the two were rivals, and while they had differing views they were by no means enemies, it is one of the best books written to describe the complicated relationship between Gandhi and Churchill.

While one of the most complicated relationships Winston Churchill ever had in his career was with Gandhi, one of the best relationships Churchill had ended up to be with Franklin Delano Roosevelt. Winston Churchill and Franklin D. Roosevelt's relationship has been discussed many times by historians, whether through websites, articles, or books. One of the best books which discusses the relationship between the two historical icons of Roosevelt and Churchill is Jon Meacham's *Franklin and Winston An Intimate Portrait of an Epic Friendship*. While most books discuss the correspondence of Churchill and Roosevelt, Meacham begins to take a more private look of the Roosevelt and Churchill, in a public and private setting. Jon Meacham's book is one of the first books to take this view of their friendship and reflect on how their friendship blossomed beyond World War Two. It is not a secret in history that many historians have credited these two individuals with helping to save the world, specifically speaking about World War Two. The two met briefly in 1917 and had a few exchanges during the 1920s and 1930s. But it was about 1939 when their relationship fully blossomed. In a nutshell, their relationship blossomed mainly through their jobs of trying the keep the world, but more specifically their nations, safe during the trails and torments of Hitler, Nazi Germany, and World War Two. It was through this that their private relationship grew. One reason that their relationship could have grown so personally is that they were both going through the same trials of World War Two. Therefore, in a very real sense, they became each other backbones, crutches, and in a sense, a safety net. They were so close that when Winston Churchill heard of the death of Franklin D. Roosevelt, Churchill contacted Roosevelt's wife, Eleanor and told her

"I have lost a dear and cherished friendship which

> *was forged in the fire of war. I trust you may find consolation in the magnitude of his work and the glory of his name."*

While Winston Churchill formed great friendships during his political career, that was definitely not all he did during this time. But to get a full grasp of his length and work in politics, we will need to take a few steps back to when he started in the early 1900s at 26 years old.

THE POLITICAL BEGINNINGS OF A POLITICAL STAR

❧

Within a year of Winston Churchill sitting in the House of Commons, he was classified as being a rising political star. One of the first steps that Churchill took in office dealt with dealings going on in the military, such as the dismissal of Major-General Sir Henry Colville as Commander-in-Chief of Gibraltar. Churchill believed that many in the government did not understand the works of the military, and therefore, Churchill stated that they should have no say in what can or cannot go on in the military during these situations. Churchill further stated that while sometimes the government must intervene in the military, these moments are few and far between. Winston Churchill also said that the reasoning for this is because, in order for the military to continue to prosper in the correct ways, it is essential that the War Department handles their own cases of dismissing and promotion without interference as this interference could hinder the war department's growth. During this time, Winston Churchill also spoke out against Mr. Brodrick's Army.

Forging ahead a few years, in 1907, Winston Churchill received a change in his political career. By this time, Churchill had continued to make waves in the political field, and many people started to feel that he would eventually see a promotion. And this he did, after his return from Africa in 1907. It was this year that King Edward and Herbert Asquith were discussing political plans, and Asquith noted that Churchill had wanted to get into the cabinet. While Winston Churchill himself did want to enter the cabinet, he wanted to do so under his post of under-secretary. However, Asquith had found, what he felt, was a better place for Winston Churchill. Asquith ended up asking Churchill if he would instead be placed in the Colonial Office, the Local Government Board or the Admiralty. Of course, Winston Churchill wanted to join the Colonial Office. However, within a month of stating his decision, Churchill was told by Asquith that he would be placed in the Board of Trade.

Of course, Winston Churchill continued on his public speaking tours. He had now even expanded his tours into other areas, such as Africa, which is where he often spoke about trades. He also continued to impress and not always impress others during his speeches and the political parties he ended up going to. One such person was Clementine Hozier, who would eventually become his wife. In her later years, Clementine was noted to say that at first Winston had made a wrong impression on her. However, over the course of the evening, he was able to win her over with his intelligence and charming personality.

※

It was also in 1908 when Winston Churchill decided to start focusing more on social changes in the world in his political career. And one reason he began to shift over to more social changes was actually that Winston also had a change of political parties in 1908. It was during this time that others were running for re-election, and due to this re-election, Winston Churchill was defeated. He then decided to switch over from conservative with semi-liberal views to completely liberal. There is no denying that part of this change was because Winston had lost his previous post and was asked to run in Dundee, which was completely liberal. However, this was not the only reason. Over the course of his political career, social changes would become one of Winston Churchill's main focuses, especially during the second world war. It would also be his fight for the good of social changes that would give the public a different view of Churchill as he could also be found volunteering and helping those less fortunate in a variety of ways. Which for many people was a good chance to see in Winston Churchill because he would often come across as not having any concern for the less fortunate due to his upbringing in a socially well-established family.

A POLITICAL FAMILY MAN

❦

Of course, not all of Winston Churchill's roles were completely public and political in nature as some of his roles were private and more family focused. Such is the case of his courting and marriage to Clementine. However, this is not to say that this more private action did not influence him on the political and public world. As was the thought of the time, people did not fully acknowledge and give bachelors enough credit as they were often thought to be unkept in ways. Therefore, through marrying Clementine, Churchill was able to also gain a little more support from the public and others in the political field.

❦

After his marriage, Churchill continued to speak about the causes that were affecting people socially, and also as a liberal, began discussing one of his father's interests which had to do with mining and David Lloyd George's The peoples' Budget.

During a time when Great Britain was being faced with an economic depression, the Liberal government came up with the idea of The Peoples' Budget, which introduced new and different taxes on Great Britain's wealthy class to support the people of the lower classes through social welfare programs. Through this time, Winston Churchill and David Lloyd George not only became political allies but also gained a personal friendship. The two fought for social change by promoting The People's Budget and working to create better economic conditions for the lower classes. The House of Commons passed the bill in 1909, but the House of Lords then blocked it. While it was passed into law a year later, it was not passed without a fight between the House of Commons and the House of Lords. Once the law was passed, Winston Churchill took tremendous pride in knowing he helped create some social change for good in the world. During the time, Churchill had said of The Peoples' Budget that he was proud of being able to help the people who were living in poverty by creating guidelines, where they could receive help and be able to live and not have to compete with anything or anyone with all of their strength.

✥

On a more private level for Winston Churchill, and his wife Clementine, it was the same year of The People's Budget in 1909 when the couple welcomed their first child. Their daughter, Diana, was born that summer on July 11th.

✥

In his early 40's, Winston Churchill once again looked at bettering the Military through his political career. It was in 1915 when Churchill began to focus on establishing the Landships Committee. One of the reasons the military once again became the focus of Churchill was because the country was now in the middle of World War One. Through his time in the military about 20 years prior and looking around at what was going on during World War One, Winston Churchill knew the military needed to be able to come up with better weapons for the front lines. Therefore, he proposed and created the Landships Committee, which was a specific British military committee which would work to develop the best-armored vehicles that could be made at the time. In the end, what would come of the Landships Committee would be what we called the tank today. While the Landships Committee started under Churchill, once it came into light by the War Office, it was the Army which took it over. The plans for the tank went into the trail on several occasions during the beginning of the year and did not officially obtain the title "Tank" until the end of that year. At first, it was named Little Willie and then went on to the name Big Willie. Another change for the committee was a name change, going from the Landships Committee to the Tank Supply Committee. And while the War Office eventually took over the creation of the tank, the whole committee would not have happened without the press of Sir Winston Churchill, which therefore means, it is because of him that the military now has an armored vehicle known as the tank.

During his political career, Winston Churchill helped his nation get through two wars, the first one being World War One. As stated above, we already knew he helped kick off the first creation of the armored tank. However, Winston Churchill did more than just start a committee which was to build armored vehicles for the front lines. When the war broke out in 1914, Winston Churchill was sitting in the seat in politics as the First Lord of the Admiralty. In 1915, after a couple of failures in his political career, Churchill resigned and instead joined the army and going back towards the front lines of World War One in 1916, however, he would still be a part of Parliament. A year later, it was Prime Minister and friend of Churchill, David Lloyd George who appointed Winston Churchill as Minister of Munitions. Winston Churchill kept this position until early 1919. After leaving this position, he took a post as the Secretary of State for Air and War, where he met with several others in Paris for the Paris Peace Conference and the discussion of what to do now that World War One was over.

WOMEN'S RIGHTS AND OTHER SOCIAL CAUSES

൦ൕ

Of course, we also cannot talk about Winston Churchill in office during the 1910s without discussing women's rights. And this can be a very complex topic in the Winston Churchill history because historians do not entirely agree on whether or not he supported women's suffrage. But before we discuss the history of Winston Churchill and Women's right to vote, it should be pointed out that women's suffrage in Britain was different from women's suffrage on the United States of America. In America, women's suffrage was a debate in the late 1800s, but for Great Britain, it was not. So when Winston Churchill wrote the private letter stating he did not support women's suffrage, most women in Great Britain also did not support women's suffrage. However, we can also look at the early 1900s and feel that through marrying Clementine, who supported women's suffrage and having a daughter, Winston Churchill's views on women's suffrage could have evolved a bit as it is stated that he did side with his wife on the views. But even with this, Winston Churchill did oppose women's suffrage in 1910 when there was a bill in Parliament that would have given women who were head of the household the chance to vote. However, it is believed that his reasons were because of the fear of conservative women using this as leverage. It is also recorded that Winston Churchill did support other rights for women. For example, Churchill was very supportive in 1918 when Parliament passed the Representation of the People's Act. This act allowed women over thirty who met the minimum property requirements to vote. However, it also allowed all men over the age of 21 to vote. Therefore, historians have debated whether Churchill was entirely for women's rights as the Representation of the People's Act also included men.

❧❦❧

However, it has also come into light that Winston Churchill was very supportive of women. Some believe this was because he always had a close relationship with his mother than his father. Therefore, it was natural for him to support women. Others state that because he was such a devoted husband and father of four daughters in the course of his life, he would naturally become more supportive of women. Other people also cite that it was just part of Winston Churchill's personality to be supportive of women because of their social status. However, another reason is simply because of the way he viewed women who he saw fighting in the military. Winston stated himself that through the years he saw women in the military, they did the same thing any male did as they would serve in hospitals, go to the front lines with the military vehicles, and above all, be moral backbones for their country. In Churchill's mind, this was a big enough reason to support women in other areas of life, such as giving them the right to vote, as long as it was done in a way that it did not threaten anyone or, as a liberal, make the conservatives stronger.

※

In 1922, after 22 years in Parliament, Winston Churchill lost and was officially out of Parliament. A little lost on what to do, Churchill decided to retire to the south of France, where he once again started to focus more on writing now that he had more time to do so. However, this retirement would not last long as Churchill continued to try to gain a seat again, which he did two years later when he won at Epping as the Independent Constitutionalist anti-Socialist and took on the role of Chancellor of the Exchequer. At the same time, Churchill also switched parties, once again becoming Conservative.

※

It was during this time as Chancellor of the Exchequer that Winston Churchill replaced the Gold Standard in Britain. Churchill, with the help of others, began to believe that this way was superior when managing money, and with a great depression, Churchill hoped it could help in the long run. He was working on his first significant budget, and he did not want to make the economy any worse off than what it already was. However, it should be noted that Churchill still did have a little anxiety over the issue of the gold standard as he still had questions. However, he gave in to the advice of others, and the gold standard was re-established.

※

Furthermore, Churchill also started to focus more on social

causes to do what he could to help better economies on a more individual level. He proposed benefits for the lower classes when it came to income taxes. He also proposed social welfare type programs at his first budget meeting, where he also proposed the re-establishment of the gold standard. These new social welfare programs included pensions for widows and their children. This plan, which would have covered more than 350,000 children and over 200,000 women, would also include any orphans. Churchill is quoted saying about the social welfare plan,

※

> *"I like the association of this new scheme of widows' pensions and earlier old-age pensions with the dying-out of the cost of the war pensions. I like to think that the sufferings, the sacrifices, the sorrow of the war have sown a seed from which a strong tree will grow, under which, perhaps many generations of British people may find shelter against some at least of the storms of life. This is far the finest war memorial you could set up to the men who gave their lives, their limits, or their health, and those who lost their dear ones in the country's cause."*

※

When Churchill was done giving his first budget speech, it was stated to be one of the best budget speeches not only by others in Parliament but also by the King.

It was also during these early to mid 1920s when Churchill began giving more speeches than before. He went back on tour, especially during the winter months, to give speeches, first of which mostly focused on defended all his proposed budget plans. At the same time, Churchill was continuing to make more waves as a politician. An example of this is when he was given special appointment to a special committee in the Cabinet. This committee was given the task to evaluate the recommendations of the work environment and conditions of the coal mines. Of course, with Winston Churchill's previous experience in the coal mines and the leadership his father, Lord Randolph, had in helping the coal mines as a statesman, Churchill was well suited for the special committee. However, it was Churchill which denied this task. Throughout the process, Churchill would find himself debating with the committee anyway as it was not long until negotiations between politicians on the committee and the coal miners and owners hit a road black as the coal miners decided to strike in 1926, which is now known as the General Strike of 1926. It was Churchill that went in front of people and supported the coal miners and owners by stating they all had a right to strike. He further instructed Parliament that once the threat of a bigger, national strike was gone, they were to go back with patience and understanding and trying to negotiate terms again. As Churchill basically told a crowd, it was the duty of the Parliament to do so for the bettering of the economy and society. Luckily, the strike did not end long, and negotiations were settled in May of that year.

❧ IV ☙
THE LATER YEARS OF SIR WINSTON CHURCHILL

❧

Continuous effort - not strength or intelligence - is the key to unlocking our potential.
Winston Churchill

❧

As stated above, it was World War Two which has always been one of Winston Churchill's biggest claims to fame, especially as a politician. It was in the 1930s when Winston Churchill started questioning Hitler and what was going on in Germany way before several other people did. In fact, while most people in England felt that Italy or Japan was a bigger threat to their nation, it was Sir Winston Churchill who began to speak out that the biggest threat he could see to England was Germany. And Winston Churchill's biggest reason in feeling that Germany was a threat was none other than Adolph Hitler as Churchill was caught saying on many occasions that if Hitler ever turned on England, it would change the air and it would take a powerful army to defend England from Hitler and Germany. Not only did Winston Churchill take a huge role in trying to warn people and countries about Hitler and Germany but he also played a huge role in the Second World War.

※

As early as 1933, Winston Churchill was trying to warn others about Germany. He would give speeches during his tours and to others in the Parliament, most of which were usually not very interested in his belief or unhappy that he would speak of such a thing. He further wrote about the threat of Germany to others in England and around the world, where he would state that what was going on in Germany was bound to turn into a war. But at this time, most people, especially in England, were worried about India. And while India was a legitimate concern for them during this period, it was not Winston Churchill's biggest concern.

※

In 1933, around the time Churchill was trying to get people in Parliament to listen to him about Hitler and Germany, he was asked to go back to India and serve on the Parliamentary Committee there. Winston Churchill turned this role down. Winston Churchill further caused an earthquake within the government when he stood up to Baldwin and the Government's India policy by leading a public movement against it. This was the moment when Churchill caused not only a split between himself and Baldwin but also within the Government.

※

Even with the split, Churchill did not give up on his push to warn others about the threat of Hitler and Germany, and he gave it an even bigger push when in later 1933 and early 1934, he learned that Germany seemed to be preparing for war. At this point, Churchill tried to push it so much that he was using nearly every one of his public appearances, including parties, to discuss the threat of war with Germany. And in a genuine sense, Churchill had to extend his ways and contacts as he was being excluded from various areas in Parliament at the time. Furthermore, he was also losing his writing contracts with the papers because, as the owners of the papers would claim, his views did not agree with the views of the majority.

THE START OF THE SECOND WORLD WAR

❦

By 1938, Winston Churchill had exhausted many of his contacts, new and old, with his push about the war coming up in Germany. However, he was still far from ever giving up on trying to convince people to prepare for another world war. Most of this was because Winston Churchill had already lived and seen a world war, the first world war, and therefore he felt more fear and knowledge of when another one could be brewing. He also knew that Great Britain's military was much weaker than Germany's army. And once he started to notice pro-German and anti-French propaganda in Britain, he took matters into his own hands and flew to France to advocate an Anglo-French alliance. And once he did this, the British Cabinet wasted no time in telling people that Winston Churchill was speaking for himself and did not share the same views of the Government. But in Winston Churchill's mind, he knew exactly what he was doing. As Churchill feared that if France broke due to the war that Hitler and Nazi Germany would be able to take over France and England, and then they would further take over other parts of the world. Therefore, in Churchill's mind, he was on one of his last resorts to stop this terror from happening as much as possible. Furthermore, Churchill believed that is countries banded together against Germany and Hitler; they would be able to defeat the Hitler and his band of Nazi's. And Winston Churchill's efforts to warn people about the dangers of Hitler and Germany would bring him all the way to World War Two.

◈

It was the first day of September in 1939 when Winston Churchill learned of Germany invading Poland. It was time where everything Churchill had said in warning of a second world war approaching was finally starting. It was also this day when the Prime Minister informed Churchill that he wanted Churchill to be part of the Government. It was only a couple days later when Winston Churchill would join the War Cabinet as First Lord of the Admiralty, which was the exact same position Churchill held during part of World War One. And Churchill wasted no time in taking the lead and trying to be involved in as much as possible. And it was all of his hard work during the next few months which led him to one of his greatest and most prominent roles during one of the world's trying times, becoming Prime Minister.

◈

Once Churchill and the Cabinet heard that Germany wanted to invade the Scandinavian countries next, such as Norway, Churchill began to contemplate ways to invade Germany. One of the ways he discussed with others was to attack the supply line of the Nazi Army. However, when this would not work out with the ones closest to him, Winston Churchill decided to head to Paris in hopes of trying to convince his allies that this is the course of action that needed to be taken against Nazi Germany and Hitler. And while Churchill was known as a convincing person with his speeches, he was unable to convince his allies and before he was able to return home, German forces had invaded the Scandinavian countries. Once again, Churchill was at his drawing table for the next move.

※

However, this time, Churchill felt that Hitler had made a mistake by invading the Scandinavian areas of Norway and Denmark because now, Churchill believes, Hitler had isolated his Nazi Army. According to Churchill, this would give the British army strength in an attack against the Nazi's.

※

It was also no secret that one of Churchill's strengths as Prime Minister during World War Two was that he had faced a previous world war and was, therefore, able to make comparisons between the two. In a sense, this was able to keep Winston Churchill ahead of the game in areas during the second world war. It was also a plus that Churchill had good sense when it came to handling situations under pressure and in times of crises. Reality is, in order to be able to successfully conquer a strong army such at Hitler's Nazi army, good sense, keen observation, ability to handle tough and dangerous situation, and be able to think on the spot when coming up with a solution would be key in being able to successfully win against the Nazi's. Winston Churchill also understood something else before many other people in the

Government did, and that was he needed to befriend the right countries, such as France, to overthrow Nazi Germany and Hitler.

※

It only took a few more months before Churchill was being asked to form a government by the King of England. By this time, Germany had invaded several areas, such as Holland, Belgium, Luxembourg, and France. The King asking this out of Winston Churchill was really no surprise to anyone. By this time, people had expected it to happen at some point. And it was not just because Winston Churchill was the Prime Minister but also because of his leadership abilities, which he had shown previously during World War One, and there were still a few people that remembered that time. Even Baldwin, who had taken a disliking to Churchill in the past had stated on more than one occasion that if a war was to arise, and it did, then it would be Churchill that would be a good lead as a war Prime Minister. There is no doubt that having the toll of the war on his shoulders was to affect Winston Churchill. It was an enormous amount of not only work but also stress, but in Churchill's fashion, he took the bull by the horns and did whatever he could to save not only his nation but also most of the world. It should be no surprise that there were many nights when Churchill did not go to bed until early in the morning, only to get up a few hours later.

※

One of Winston Churchill's most famous moments of World War Two was when Churchill found out that Hitler was on his way to France for their surrender. It was at this moment that Winston Churchill was quoted saying,

> *"Let us, therefore, brace ourselves to our duty and so bear ourselves that if the British Empire and its Commonwealth last for a thousand years, men will still say, 'This was their finest hour'."*

It is no hidden message that if you have read or done any research on Winston Churchill, you read the words "finest hour" regularly. There are several books which reference this statement, including Winston Churchill's own book from his Second World War series, *Their Finest Hour*, which is volume 2. It was basically Winston Churchill stating it was time for England to enter into the war as they could not let their allies go down without a fight. And, more importantly, Winston Churchill knew that it was England which would be next on the list and he was going to do everything in his power not to let Hitler and his Nazi German forces take control of England.

※

It was the summer of 1940 when Great Britain was waiting for the German invasion. The date when it officially happened was July 10th. It was on this date the Luftwaffe made its first large-scale bombing raid against Britain in the air. It was 6 days later when Hitler issued the Sea Lion, which was a landing operation against Britain. However, Hitler would have to battle the plans in which Winston Churchill had devised by the time Hitler started to enter England, as by this time, Churchill was also in a defensively aggressive mood towards Hitler and the Nazis. It was also around this time where Churchill had advised everyone he could that they would need to side with the United States of America to officially win this war and overthrow Hitler and his Nazis. Winston Churchill furthermore stated about becoming friends with the United States that they would do it at all cost. This would also lead to one of Winston Churchill's most famous friendships, the one with the United States President Franklin D. Roosevelt. However, at this time, Churchill was nothing thinking about becoming personal friends with an American, he was thinking of his nation becoming friends with the United States of America as a whole.

CHURCHILL AND THE 1940S

During World War Two, Churchill was known to make the decisions he felt was right and not the decision that the Parliament or Government would tell him, whether through policies or otherwise, was right. One such example of this was when Winston Churchill told the Duke of Windsor not to return to his home and to basically not have a view about Hitler, Nazi Germany, or anything involved with World War Two. Through this time, and before the start of the war, Churchill had a pretty good relationship with the King and Queen of England, and therefore, Churchill giving such orders was noted by them as a quick gesture. However, the king and queen were known to get a little annoyed by some of Winston Churchill's manners, claiming that he would show up late when planning to visit them and could often come off as a bit rude. However, like most people, they learned to work around this part of Winston Churchill's personality because he was also very kind and considerate. On top of that, he was highly intelligent and a great leader. And like everyone in the world, Churchill is going to have some flaws in his personality.

❧

It was in August of 1940 when Churchill's bud dying up to the United States of American began to pay off for the advantage of both countries. On the 10th of that month, President Roosevelt contacted Churchill and told him that if they would let the states use naval and air bases on British soil and, if necessary, promised to send the British fleet to other parts of the Empire, they Britain would be able to use aircraft and destroyers from the states. Winston Churchill accepted these terms without a thought because, in his mind, if the United States were on the side of England, then Nazi Germany and Hitler would eventually see an end. In Churchill's mind, there were no Ifs, ANDs or BUTs about this, it is just how it was going to be.

❧

In September of that year, Hitler decided to postpone Operation Sea Lion. While there is no set of reasons why, about a month before this, Hitler had sent off several bombs to the London streets, which terrorized and destroyed many parts of the city. It was Winston Churchill that went to see the horrifying remains and, upon his arrival, was greeted with enthusiasm and praise by people who knew he would come and continued to give him words of encouragement in doing everything necessary to beat Hitler and Nazi Germany. Wither this and other factors, such as The United States of America now working with England cause Hitler to postpone the Sea Lion remains to be unknown. However, anything is possible at this point.

❧

Even though operation Sea Lion was canceled, this did not mean that there was no longer a threat aimed at England from Hitler and Germany as bombing had started. Furthermore, this threat was made more evident in September of 1940 when Germany, Japan, and Italy signed a pact. While Winston Churchill knew that this could mean more danger for Great Britain, he did not let the agreement affect his work. If anything, it made Churchill more determined than ever to win the war and beat Germany and Hitler once and for all. And he was not shy in telling people what he thought, even with the pact in place.

❧

Near the end of 1940, there seemed to be nearly constant bombing going on between Great Britain and England. Throughout this time, Winston Churchill would often discuss how the mistakes of World War One could not be made again. He further still believed that no matter what people thought, he knew that they would be able to obtain victory. However, he still felt that they were only capable of this with the help of the United States of America. Churchill also felt there was something else needed to help aid Britain in the victory. This was when Winston Churchill began to realize that submarines would be more important than bombs. This is another moment when the United States of America would step in.

❧

The end of 1940 and the beginning of 1941 show that Winston Churchill and United States of America President

Franklin D. Roosevelt remained in close contact. Roosevelt agreed to give Churchill and Britain the tools they needed to finish off the war. However, Churchill was worried about how they would be able to repay the United States back for their services. By the summer of 1941, Churchill was preparing and waiting for a German invasion in September of that year, which he wrote to Roosevelt about. It was time for both Winston Churchill and President Roosevelt to meet in person. Therefore, in August of that year, Winston boarded a ship and headed to Placentia Bay, Newfoundland for the Atlantic Conference to do just that.

ॐ

Part of Winston Churchill hoped that when the world noted he had met with Present Roosevelt, Germany would back off on their invasion. While Churchill did not get the United States to declare war, Roosevelt did tell Churchill that the United States of America would wage war and that they fully supported the Churchill and his nation. Then it was the Prime Minister and the President who came up with the Atlantic Charter, which showed they were together in taking down Hitler and Nazi Germany. A few days later, Churchill admitted that the meeting was highly symbolic during the war, as it meant that the English speaking nations were unified in this battle.

ॐ

It would just be a couple of months later when World War Two would include the biggest historical moments in the history of World War Two. On December 7th of 1941, the Japanese had attacked America at Pearl Harbor. Reportedly, Churchill was with an American Ambassador when they received word of the attack over the radio. Immediately, Churchill said they would wage war on Japan. He then called up Roosevelt to tell him that he fully backed the United States and he would make sure that his nation would do everything in their power to help the United States of American in their time, just as the United States has been helping Britain.

※

Less than a week later, Winston Churchill began heading to America to meet up with President Roosevelt. While Roosevelt was okay with meeting later, it was Winston Churchill who wanted to meet with Roosevelt as soon as possible so that a couple of things could be established. The first item on Churchill's list was the naval situation between Europe and the United States of America. The second item on the list was both British and American military leaders meeting to establish a plan to defeat Hitler and Nazi German and officially win World War Two. On December 22, Roosevelt and Churchill met to discuss these points and other items at what came to be known as the Arcadia Conference.

※

Afterward, Churchill went off to Canada to conduct business there and then came back to meet up with Roosevelt and sign the United Nations Charter. In the middle of January, after vacationing and meeting with other politicians, in Florida, Churchill went back to Britain to meet with the War Cabinet where he would update them on all his work done in the United States of America and Canada, specifically Churchill spoke about the meeting with President Roosevelt. During the meeting with the war cabinet, Churchill said that Roosevelt to him that they could trust him. Churchill further told the war cabinet that Roosevelt will not lead them wrong and that he can be trusted. Churchill then spoke to the King and Queen and told them that he knew Roosevelt could be trusted until the very end and that he was sure that Britain would end up victorious in this war.

※

It was also during this time when Franklin D. Roosevelt and Winston Churchill were becoming personal friends. One example of their personal friendship growing was not only the trust they placed in each other, especially when it came to Winston Churchill trusting Roosevelt but also, they were known to correspond to each other frequently. And it did not always have to deal with the war going on. For instance, they would often send each other birthday wishes.

※

Another way we can see the personal friendship between Winston Churchill and Roosevelt growing is the correspondence between the two when Churchill began struggling with his health. It was at the end of 1941 when Churchill started meeting with his doctor to discuss his health concerns. However, Churchill also would often keep the findings between him and the doctor. That was until people started to notice a physical change in Churchill. His daughter Mary started to discuss how her father seemed sad. His wife began to talk of his health declining. And Churchill began to open up to Roosevelt in explaining the reasons why his health was declining, whether it was psychological or physical in nature. However, when it came to the public and having to speak,

Churchill never missed a beat. He spoke with the same confidence while his health was declining that he did when he first started in politics.

※

In 1943, Churchill once again made a trip to the United States of America to speak in front of the United States Congress. At the end of World War Two, this speech would be on the top of the list of one of Winston Churchill's most famous speeches. This speech would become known as Churchill's fighting speech, in which he told the United States of America that Great Britain supported them in their battle against Japan. Today, this speech can be heard on the internet. In the statement, Churchill is quoted saying,

※

"And here let me say: let no one suggest that we British have not at least as great an interest as the United States in the unflinching and relentless waging of war against Japan. But I am here to tell you that we will wage that war side by side with you, in accordance with the best strategic employment of our forces..."

※

Later in 1943, while Winston Churchill started making the postwar plans for Great Britain, he headed to Casablanca. It was here where the leaders of Great Britain and the leaders of the United States of America would come together to form their plan of invasion on the European content. For weeks, the leaders of the two nations met and formed plans and contracts. For example, Roosevelt and Churchill agreed to send support to the American forces stationed in China, how they were going to build up American forces in Great Britain, and a trip to Sicily. While they discussed many subjects throughout the weeks, one of the most important was the decision to state that the only term in which the allies would accept the end of the war was unconditional surrender. While Winston Churchill agreed to this term, he was not completely supportive of the term. However, as Churchill always did during the time of World War Two; he was confident that they would win.

※

It is important to note that throughout World War Two, especially in the later years where the stress for Churchill was highest, and he was not always in the best of health, he took time for his family. As noted before, Churchill was a family man, and this was proven during 1944 when he went to see his grandchildren in London. Upon his return, he was noted talking about them and discussing how the world that they were living in now was not a world he wanted for his grandchildren. It is believed that this was another reason to bring an end to World War Two. Winston Churchill wanted to see his children and grandchildren live in the best world as possible.

※

In early 1945, Winston Churchill was able to nearly smell victory in World War Two. He knew the end was near and it was in his favor. It was during this time where Churchill began to travel to several different areas in the world. He met with Roosevelt and Stalin where they all signed the Yalta

Agreement, which discussed the Anglo-American relationship with the Soviets. He further traveled to places such as Poland, Greece, and Egypt while working on finalizing the war. Of course, he was not always sure and sometimes was a bit anxious about the way he would be treated in these nations. However, Winston Churchill had little issue with them, and he was sometimes surprised by the good treatment he received from not only the leaders of the specific nations but the citizens as well.

※

In April of 1945, Hitler was killed. One of Winston Churchill's most prominent enemies and one of the leading causes of World War Two was dead. It was then when Churchill would do the celebrations as much as he could while continuing to work out the loose ends of World War Two. No matter how Churchill felt about the celebrations, he was like a celebrity in Britain. For one celebration, Winston Churchill went to the Palace where the King and Queen spoke of their praise and then it was like a parade. Churchill drove around in an open car, shaking hands and waving to the citizens of England. And then, of course, there was Winston Churchill's famous victory speech on the balcony overlooking the Whitehall. When Winston Churchill went up to speak, people were in awe and joyous of his speech. It is this speech that also proves Churchill's personality did not change in the war. He was still the humble, pleasant, and well-spoken man he always had been as he told the crowd that this was their victory.

THE RETIREMENT YEARS OF CHURCHILL

❧

Now in his 70s, Winston Churchill was beginning to slow down. At the end of 1940, Winston Churchill took time away from being Prime Minister of the United Kingdom. During this time, Churchill took a lot of vacations, spent as much time as he could with his family, wrote various books, and did a few things in the office. However, he once again became Prime Minister in 1951. During his next five years as Prime Minister, he put the same heart in soul into his job as he did the first time. However, this was not always met with the same praise. There were several decisions that Churchill made during his last few years in office that did not find people well. However, Churchill took the criticism has he always had done and in 1955, he retired from the political world.

❧

By now, Churchill was in his eighties, and both he and his

wife were suffering from their own illnesses. There were several times in the early 1960s when people felt that Winston Churchill was near his deathbed. During these years Churchill not only fought various illness like pneumonia but he also fell and broke his hip. Within the last couple years of his life, most of the time Winston Churchill was kept to his bed. That was until January 24, 1965, when Sir Winston Churchill passed away. During his funeral, which you can still see on the internet today, his wife, Clementine called the service a triumph and not a funeral. And there is no way to debate her on this statement. While Winston Churchill was known to be a man with a quick and sometimes short temper, he might have also been known to be humble and kind one minute and then barking orders the next; he was one of the most cherished people of his time. The time and work Winston Churchill put into taking care of his nation and the time and work he put into bringing victory during World War Two is more amazing than what he gets credit for. Winston Churchill took an amazing lead as Prime Minister of the United Kingdom during World War Two from trying to warn everyone that Hitler and Nazi Germany was something to look out for to becoming Allies with the United States of America. There are not a lot of people in this world, during Winston Churchill's time or the present time, that could think, act, and react the same ways Churchill did.

V
CONCLUSION

❦

My most brilliant achievement was my ability to be able to persuade my wife to marry me.
Winston Churchill

❦

Since Winston Churchill passed away, historians have been writing about him and discussing the many different areas he dealt with throughout his life. This is not only proven in the countless academic articles that are written about Winston Churchill but also the hundreds of books that have been written about the man since the late 1900s.

❦

Winston Churchill was a complicated man in many ways who held great strengths and weaknesses during his lifetime. One of his greatest strengths was being able to remain calm in times of crisis. This was shown time and time again during his political career, especially during World War Two. Observation was another great strength of Winston Churchill. And if it were not for this observation, he would not have been able to prepare for World War Two as he did. Churchill knew before anyone else he communicated with that a second world war was coming and much of his knowings came from simple observation on what was going on in Germany with Hitler and the Nazis. Another one of Churchill's strength was his passion. During his military years, political decades, and as a family man, Churchill was very passionate about the hats he wore in his life. He wanted to do his bests in every situation and always gave everything he had to his role at the time.

~ ∞ ~

Unfortunately, sometimes his strengths could also hold a weakness of Winston Churchill, especially when it came to being a family man. While he tried to create as much time as possible with his family, he was often taken away from them for various reasons during his political years. Another weakness of Winston Churchill was communication. While he believed in good communication, he did not always know how to communicate in the right way, which is one reason he often made enemies during his political years.

~ ∞ ~

We can take a lot from Sir Winston Churchill when we look at his strengths. For example, observation of the world around us can help protect us, as Churchill tried to do when he started warning of the war that was brewing in Germany. But most importantly, being able to remain calm in times of crisis is one of the most exceptional qualities anyone can have. When you read about Winston Churchill, take note of the way he remained calm in times of crisis. Note that he not only did this so he could think more clearly about the decisions he was making but he also did it for those around him. Winston Churchill knew people were looking up to him and depended on him and he was not going to let them down. And he didn't, whether he was on vacation or trying to do his best during a time of crisis.

❧ VI ☙
FOR FURTHER READING...

❦

The Last Lion by William Manchester.

❦

Churchill: A Life by Martin Gilbert.

❦

God and Churchill: How the Great Leader's Sense of Divine Destiny Changed His Troubled World and Offers Hope for Ours by Jonathan Sandys and Wallace Henley.

❦ VII ❦
BIBLIOGRAPHY

❦

Catherwood, Christopher. *Winston Churchill: the flawed genius of World War II*. New York: Berkley Caliber, 2010.

❦

Churchill, Winston. *The Second World War*. New York: Time, Inc., 1959.

❦

Churchill, Winston. *Memoirs of the Second World War: an abridgment of the six volumes of the Second World War*. Boston: Houghton Mifflin, 1991.

❦

Herman, Arthur. Gandhi & Churchill: *the epic rivalry that destroyed an empire and forged our age*. New York: Bantam Books, 2009.

☙❧

Langworth, Richard M. *Winston Churchill, myth and reality: what he actually did and said.* Jefferson, NC: McFarland et Company, Inc., Publishers, 2017.

☙❧

Meacham, Jon. *Franklin and Winston An Intimate Portrait of an Epic Friendship.* Paw Prints, 2008.

☙❧

Russell, Douglas S. Winston Churchill, *soldier the military life of a gentleman at war.* London: Conway Maritime, 2006. Accessed February 2, 2018.

☙❧

Toye, Richard. *Winston Churchill Politics, Strategy and Statecraft.* London: Bloomsbury Publishing PLC, 2017.

YOUR FREE EBOOK!

As a way of saying thank you for reading our book, we're offering you a free copy of the below eBook.

Happy Reading!

GO WWW.THEHISTORYHOUR.COM/CLEO/

Made in the USA
Middletown, DE
05 August 2018